Vol 1

LEARNER'S DRIVING MANUAL

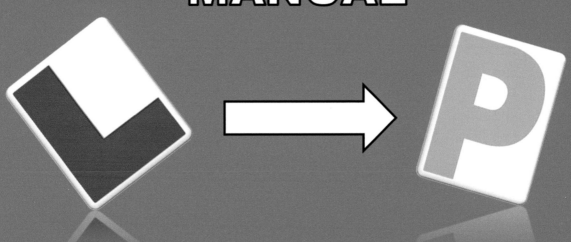

PATRICK ONANA

AuthorHouse™ UK
1663 Liberty Drive
Bloomington, IN 47403   USA
www.authorhouse.co.uk
UK TFN: 0800 0148641 (Toll Free inside the UK)
UK Local: 02036 956322 (+44 20 3695 6322 from outside the UK)

Because of the dynamic nature of the Internet, any web addresses or links contained in this book may have changed
since publication and may no longer be valid. The views expressed in this work are solely those of the author and do
not necessarily reflect the views of the publisher, and the publisher hereby disclaims any responsibility for them.

Any people depicted in stock imagery provided by Getty Images are models,
and such images are being used for illustrative purposes only.
Certain stock imagery © Getty Images.

This book is printed on acid-free paper.

ISBN: 978-1-6655-8929-1 (sc)
ISBN: 978-1-6655-8928-4 (e)

Print information available on the last page.

Published by AuthorHouse 06/07/2021

authorHOUSE

INTRODUCTION

This book will help you learn and remember the key points of every lesson you have with your Hub n Pat Driving School instructor and to understand and retain the knowledge as you prepare for your practical driving test.

We offer a structured approach for memorizing the key points of every topic and understanding the requirements of the Driving Standards Agency, who will conduct all driving tests.

Eleven complete and fully illustrated lessons cover all the elements on which you will be assessed during your driving test. Each lesson includes:

- Detailed colour illustrations of the focus areas
- Review questions to help you assess your knowledge
- A 'facts to know' section that highlights the important information
- The most common driving faults to avoid

This book has been structured to take you from the level of novice to meeting the required standards and beyond. It is designed to help you understand what is expected from a learner driver so that you can learn more quickly. You will need fewer lessons, and will save you money.

You only fail when you stop trying!

CONTENTS

	Lessons Subjects	Keys Points
1	Mirrors view	• Interior mirror • Exterior mirror • Blind spots
2	Moving off / Stopping	• POM routine • MSM routine
3	Junctions	• MSPSL routine • Priority • Different types of junctions
4	Crossroads	• Different types of crossroads • Priority
5	Clutch control/ Half clutch	• Different level of Biting point • Coasting • When to use half clutch
6	Meetings	• Priority • MSM routine • LADA (Look-Assess-Decide-Act)
7	Progress	• Adequate clearance • Normal driving position • Pedestrian crossings
8	Roundabouts	• Priority • MSPSL routine • Left turn • Straight ahead • Right turn • Lane discipline
9	Dual carriageway	• lanes • speed • Centre reservation • Slip road
10	Anticipation skills	• Tunnel vision
11	Manoeuvres	• Parallel parking - Parking om the right • Forward bay - Reverse bay parking • Emergency stop

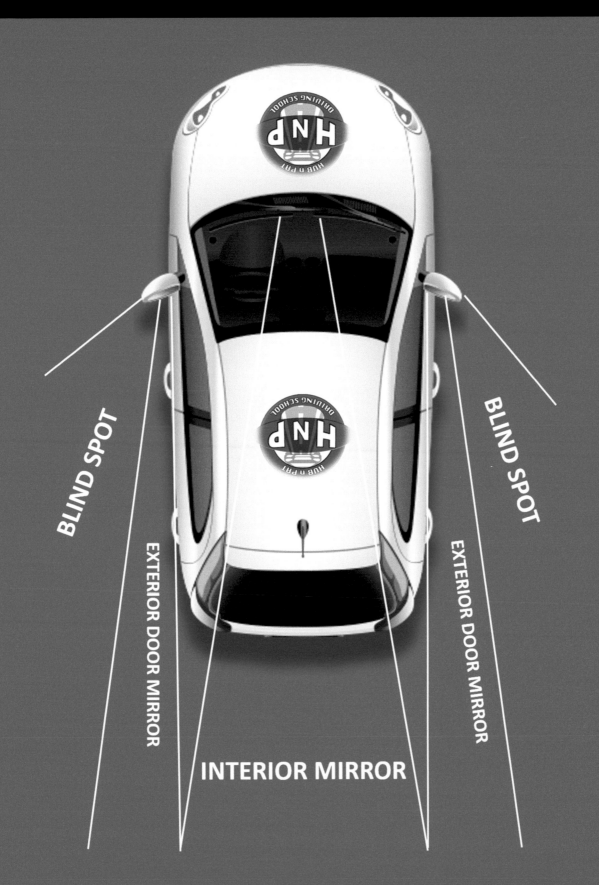

CENTRE MIRROR OR REAR-VIEW MIRROR

This mirror is made of flat glass. It gives you a true view. It enables you to see vehicles driving behind you and to estimate their speed and how far they are from you.

Side mirrors or wing mirrors

These mirrors are made of convex glass, which means things appear far away and small. These mirrors enable drivers to see what's on the sides of the vehicle, such as pedestrians, cyclists, and other vehicles.

Blind spot

A blind spot is an area not covered by mirrors.

MOVING OFF AND STOPPING

POM Routine	**MSM** Routine
Prepare - Observe - Move	Mirror – Signal - Manoeuvre

- Moving off
- Stopping
- Blind spots
- Reference point
- SCALP (safe, convenient, and legal place)

MOVING OFF

REVIEW

1. What routine do you use for moving off and what do the letters stand for?
2. What is the difference between the centre and side mirror?
3. What is a blind spot?
4. Where do you start your observation? On the least dangerous or most dangerous side?
5. When should you signal when moving off?

FACTS TO KNOW—POM ROUTINE: PREPARE—OBSERVE—MOVE!

- **Prepare**: Clutch down, first gear, find the bite
- **Observe**: Left blind spot, left mirror, centre mirror, right mirror, and right blind spot
- Signal if necessary
- **Move**: Disengage the handbrake and gradually take your foot off the clutch

TYPICAL FAULTS

- ❖ Setting too much gas
- ❖ Being too quick or too slow getting the bite
- ❖ Stalling by not balancing gas and clutch
- ❖ Signalling incorrectly
- ❖ Not fully disengaging the handbrake
- ❖ Not turning the head enough when checking blind spots

STALLING

Info's

- ❖ Holding the parking brake too long
- ❖ Releasing the clutch too quickly
- ❖ Not enough or too much bite
- ❖ Not enough acceleration

MOVING OFF

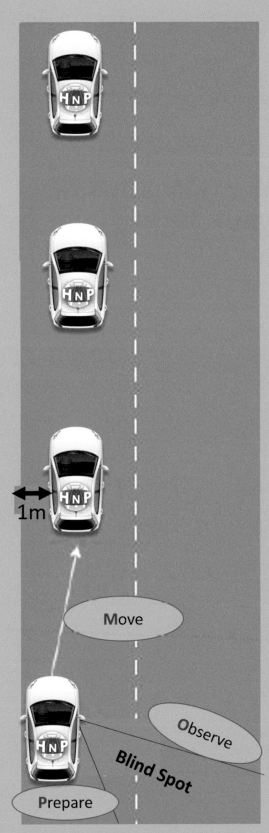

1m

MOVE

Move

OBSERVE

Observe

Blind Spot

Prepare

PREPARE

5

STOPPING

REVIEW

1. What routine do you use for stopping, and what does it stand for?
2. Which mirror do you look when stopping?
3. What signal do you put when stopping?
4. What does *manoeuvre* mean?
5. When should you signal when stopping?

FACTS TO KNOW—MSM ROUTINE: MIRROR—SIGNAL—MANOEUVRE

- **Mirror**: Centre and left mirror.
- **Signal**: Left signal.
- **Manoeuvre**: Cover the brake, clutch down, move over to the left
- Secure the vehicle: Engage the handbrake, gear to neutral, cancel signal

TYPICAL FAULTS

- ❖ Checking wrong mirrors
- ❖ Signalling incorrectly
- ❖ Putting clutch down first
- ❖ Braking with the wrong foot
- ❖ Stopping too far from or too close to the kerb
- ❖ Taking feet off pedals before securing the car
- ❖ Not fully engaging the handbrake
- ❖ Stopping somewhere illegal and inconvenient
- ❖ Coasting

COASTING

- ❖ Coasting is driving too far with the clutch down.
- ❖ With no engine braking, you can't control the speed of the vehicle.

STOPPING

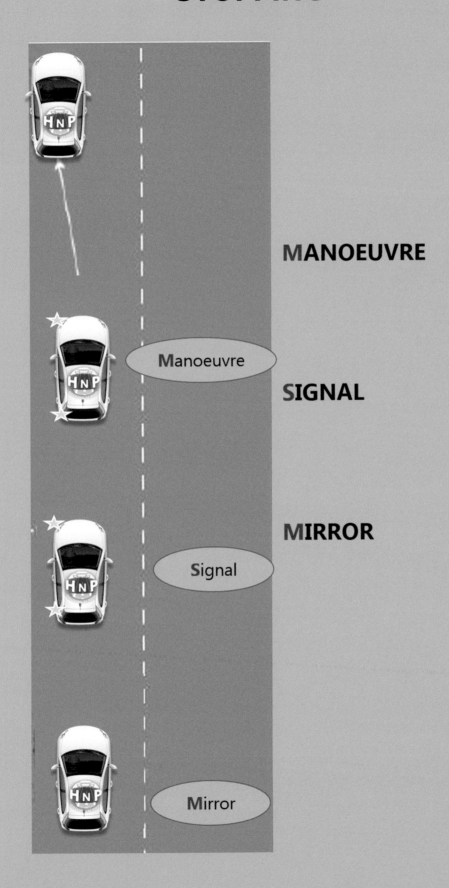

MANOEUVRE

SIGNAL

MIRROR

JUNCTIONS

MSPSL ROUTINE
Mirror – Signal – Position – Speed – Look

- Different types of junctions
- Emerging T-junctions
- Approaching junctions
- Closed and open junctions

T junction (close)

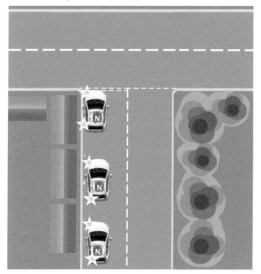

T junction (open)

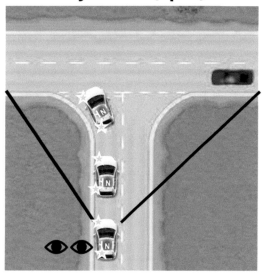

Unmarked junction

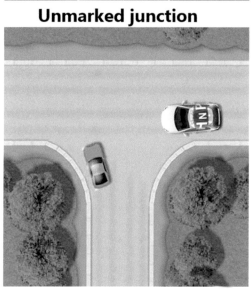

Staggered junction

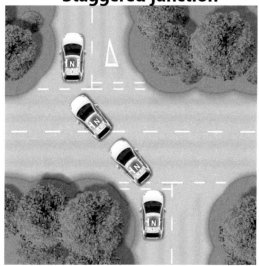

Y junction

Traffic light junction

T junction (closed)

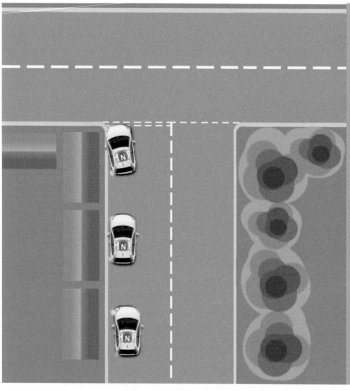

At a closed junction, you cannot see the traffic from one side or both sides because your view is obstructed by houses, trees, vehicles, or other things.

You must stop and observe before emerging.

T junction (open)

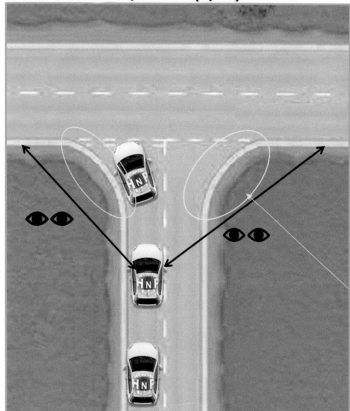

In an open junction, you can see the traffic in the distance on both sides. If there are no oncoming vehicles, you can emerge carefully.

You can recognise open junctions by the curve of the kerb.

EMERGING LEFT: T-JUNCTION

REVIEW

1. What is a junction?
2. Who has priority at a junction?
3. What does *emerging* mean?
4. When you turn left, what routine do you use on the approach?
5. Which mirrors do you check when turning left?
6. At how many car lengths do you check your mirrors?
7. Which signal do you use when turning left?
8. At how many car lengths do you use your signal?
9. Where should you position the car when turning left?
10. What speed do you use when emerging a junction?
11. Where do you stop when emerging a junction?
12. Where do you start looking when emerging left, and what is the minimum number of times to look?
13. On the new road, which mirror do you check and why?

FACTS TO KNOW—MSPSL ROUTINE: MIRRORS—SIGNAL—POSITION—SPEED—LOOK

- **Mirrors**: Centre and left mirror—eight car lengths
- **Signal**: Left signal—six car lengths
- **Position**: Normal (one metre away from kerb)
- **Speed**: 10–15 mph, first gear (open junction—stay in second gear)
- **Look**: Right—left—right (*three* times minimum)

TYPICAL FAULTS

- Not using routine on approach
- Coasting
- Approaching too fast or too slowly
- Steering too late or too early
- Not recognising closed and open junctions
- Poor observations
- Bad judgement of vehicle speed
- Stopping far behind the give way line or going over the give way line
- After turning, too slow to progress and not checking mirrors
- Not anticipating pedestrians' actions

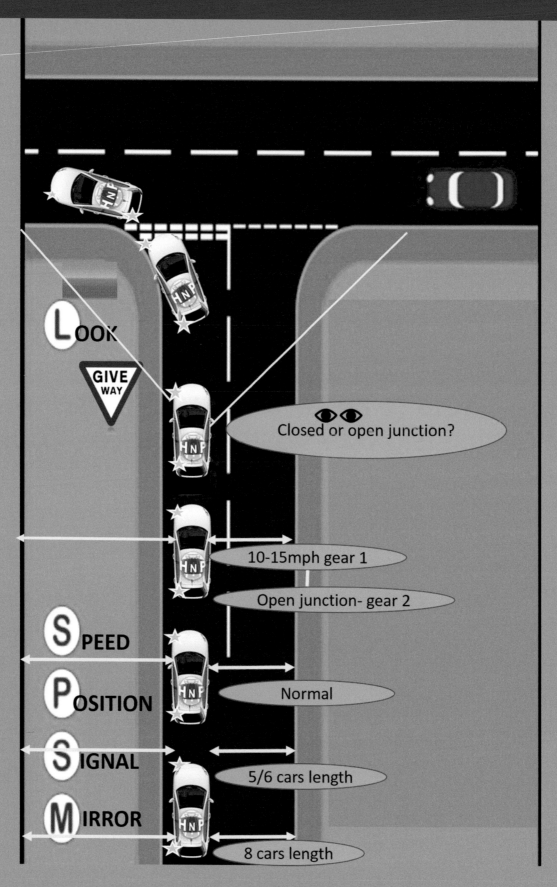

EMERGING RIGHT—T-JUNCTION

REVIEW

1. When you turn right, what routine do you use on the approach?
2. Which mirrors do you check when turning right?
3. Which signal do you use when turning right?
4. Where should you position the car when turning right?
5. What speed do you use when emerging into a junction?
6. Where do you stop when emerging into a junction?
7. Where do you start looking when emerging right and what is the minimum look? (Why?)
8. On the new road which mirror do you check and why?

FACTS TO KNOW—MSPSL ROUTINE: MIRRORS—SIGNAL—POSITION—SPEED—LOOK

- **Mirrors**: Centre and right mirror—eight car lengths
- **Signal**: Right signal—six car lengths
- **Position**: To the right (close to white line)
- **Speed**: 10–15 mph, first gear (open junction—stay in second gear)
- **Look**: Left-right-left- right—left (*five* times minimum)

TYPICAL FAULTS

- ❖ Not using routine on approach
- ❖ Coasting
- ❖ Approaching too fast or too slowly
- ❖ Steering too late or too early
- ❖ Not recognising closed or open junctions
- ❖ Poor observations
- ❖ Bad judgement of vehicle speed
- ❖ Stopping far behind the give way line or going over the give way line
- ❖ After turning, too slow to progress and not checking mirrors
- ❖ Not anticipating pedestrians' actions
- ❖ Right turn

 **SAFETY REMINDERS**

Most junctions are closed when you are emerging right.
It is very important to assess the speed of vehicles from the main road before emerging because it will take you longer to cross the path.

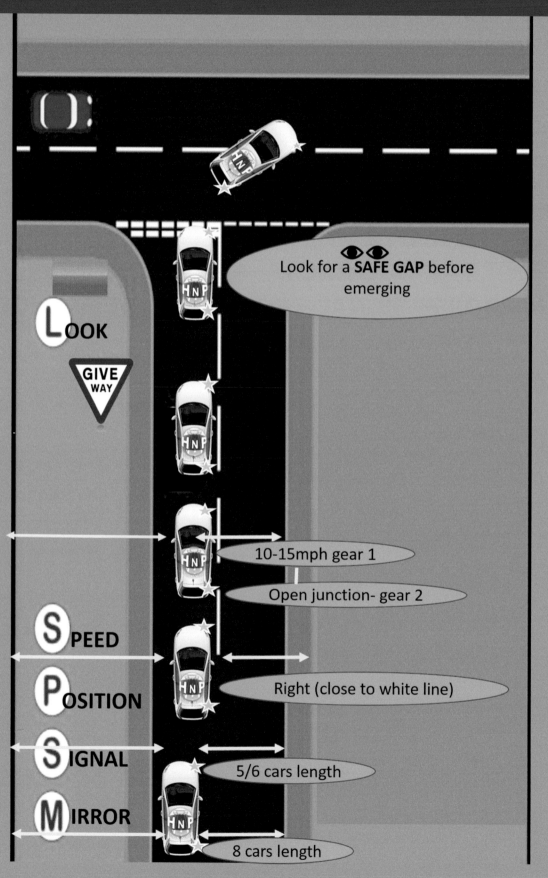

Look for a **SAFE GAP** before emerging

LOOK

GIVE WAY

10-15mph gear 1

Open junction- gear 2

SPEED

POSITION

Right (close to white line)

SIGNAL

5/6 cars length

MIRROR

8 cars length

APPROACHING A LEFT JUNCTION

REVIEW

1. What does approaching a junction means?
2. Who has priority?
3. What gear and speed do you use when approaching a junction?
4. Where do you position the vehicle when approaching a left junction?
5. Where do you look when approaching a left junction?
6. Who has priority if a pedestrian starts to cross the road when you driving along?

FACTS TO KNOW—MSPSL ROUTINE: MIRROR—SIGNAL—POSITION—SPEED—LOOK

- **Mirror**: Centre and left mirror
- **Signal**: Left signal
- **Position**: Normal (one metre away from kerb)
- **Speed**: 15–20 mph, second gear
- **Look**: Left

TYPICAL FAULTS

❖ Not using MSPSL routine on approach
❖ Forgetting who has priority
❖ Coasting
❖ Approaching too fast or too slow
❖ Steering too late or too early
❖ Not looking into the road before turning
❖ Incorrect positioning
❖ Steering wide (right) before steering left
❖ After turning, not checking mirrors, slow to progress
❖ Forgetting to cancel signal

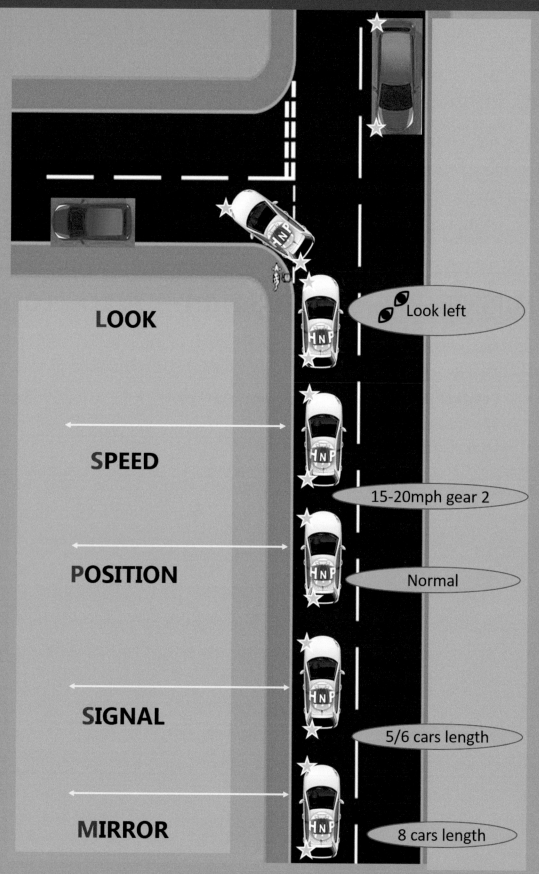

LOOK

Look left

SPEED

15-20mph gear 2

POSITION

Normal

SIGNAL

5/6 cars length

MIRROR

8 cars length

APPROACHING A RIGHT JUNCTION

REVIEW

1. Who has priority when approaching right turn?
2. Which mirrors do you check?
3. Which signal do you use?
4. What gear and speed do you use when approaching a right turn?
5. Where do you stop if there is an oncoming vehicle?
6. Where is your point of turn?
7. What is a safe gap?
8. How do you judge a safe gap?
9. Who has priority if a pedestrian starts to cross the road when you driving along?

FACTS TO KNOW—MSPSL ROUTINE:
MIRROR—SIGNAL—POSITION—SPEED—LOOK

- **Mirror:** Centre and right mirror
- **Signal:** Right signal
- **Position:** To the right (close to centre line)
- **Speed:** 15–20 mph, second gear
- **Look:** Right before moving

TYPICAL FAULTS

- ❖ Not using MSPSL routine on approach
- ❖ Coasting
- ❖ Approaching too fast or too slowly
- ❖ Steering too late or too early
- ❖ Cutting corner when turning
- ❖ Looking straight ahead when turning right
- ❖ Incorrect positioning
- ❖ After turning, not checking mirrors, slow to progress
- ❖ Forgetting to cancel signal
- ❖ Not judging the gap safely when crossing traffic

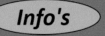 **HOW TO JUDGE A SAFE GAP**

If you can walk across, you can drive across!

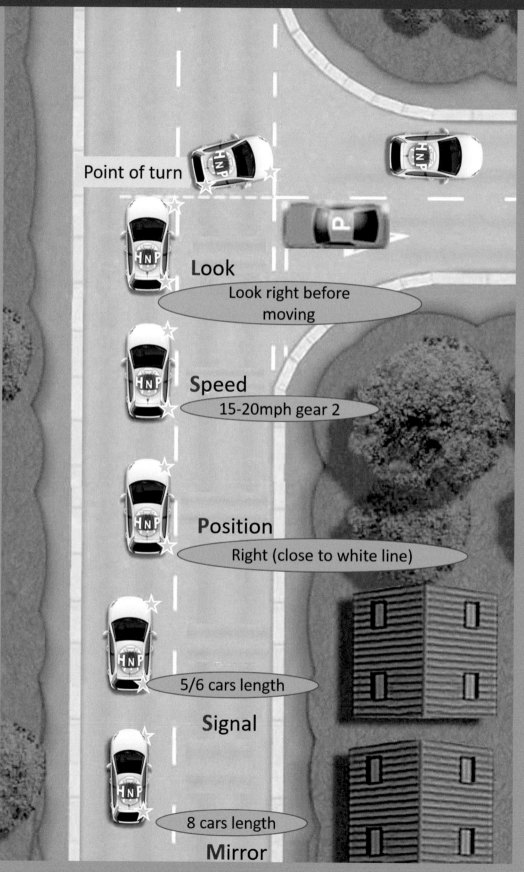

Point of turn

Look

Look right before moving

Speed

15-20mph gear 2

Position

Right (close to white line)

5/6 cars length

Signal

8 cars length

Mirror

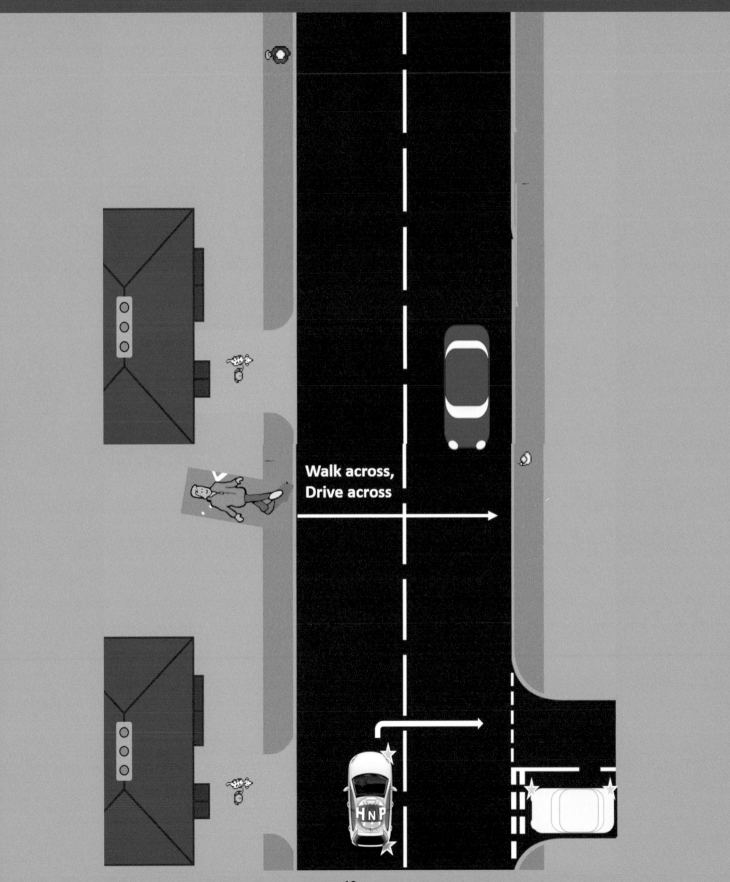

Walk across,
Drive across

CROSSROADS

DIFFERENT TYPES OF CROSSROADS:

- Marked
- Unmarked
- Controlled
- Filter Lane
- Point of Turn

MARKED CROSSROADS

REVIEW

1. What is a marked crossroad?
2. What is unmarked crossroad?
3. Who has priority on marked crossroad?
4. What routine do you use on crossroad?
5. When turning right from a major road to minor road, who has priority if there is incoming traffic and where?
6. Where do you look when emerging a marked junction?

FACTS TO KNOW

- Priority: Main road vehicles
- Routine: MSPSL routine
- Obversation: Look right, centre, left, centre, right. Keep looking, peep and creep if necessary.

TYPICAL FAULTS

- ❖ Forgetting who has priority
- ❖ Not stopping to observe when going ahead
- ❖ Poor judgment
- ❖ Incorrect positioning
- ❖ Not recognising crossroads on major road when going straight ahead

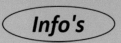 **HOW TO JUDGE A SAFE GAP**

When emerging, judge the speed and distance of traffic.
Don't make drivers change speed or direction.

MARKED AND UNMARKED CROSSROADS

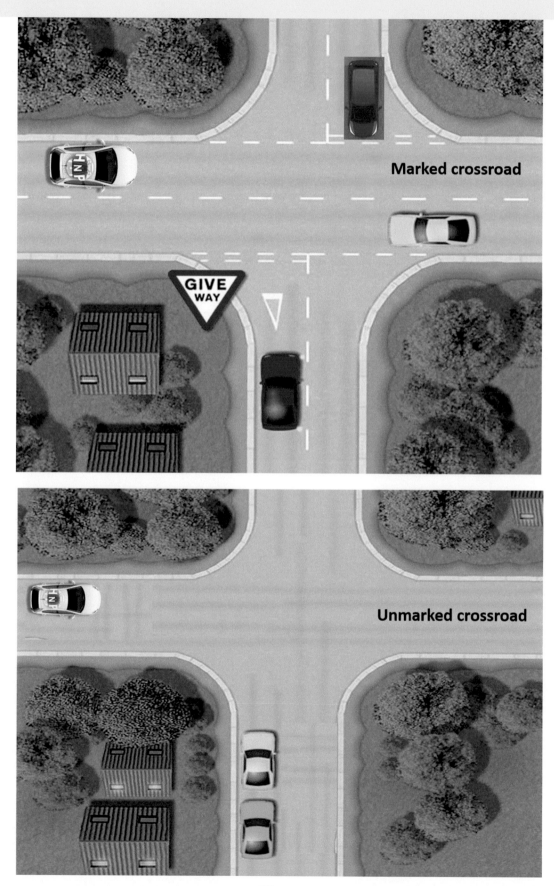

Marked crossroad

Unmarked crossroad

CONTROLLED CROSSROADS AND FILTER LANES

REVIEW

1. What is a controlled crossroad?
2. Who has priority on a controlled crossroad?
3. When turning right from a major to minor road, who has priority if there is oncoming traffic?
4. Where do you position your vehicle when turning right and why?
5. When can you wait on a yellow box junction?
6. What a filter lane?
7. Who has priority on a filter lane?

FACTS TO KNOW

- Priority: Green light has priority
- Routine: MSPSL routine
- Position when turning right: A bit to the right
- Yellow box junction: You can wait on the yellow box junction only if your exit is clear.

TYPICAL FAULTS

- ❖ Forgetting who has priority when turning right
- ❖ Poor judgment of traffic when turning right
- ❖ Incorrect positioning when turning right

YELLOW BOX JUNCTION

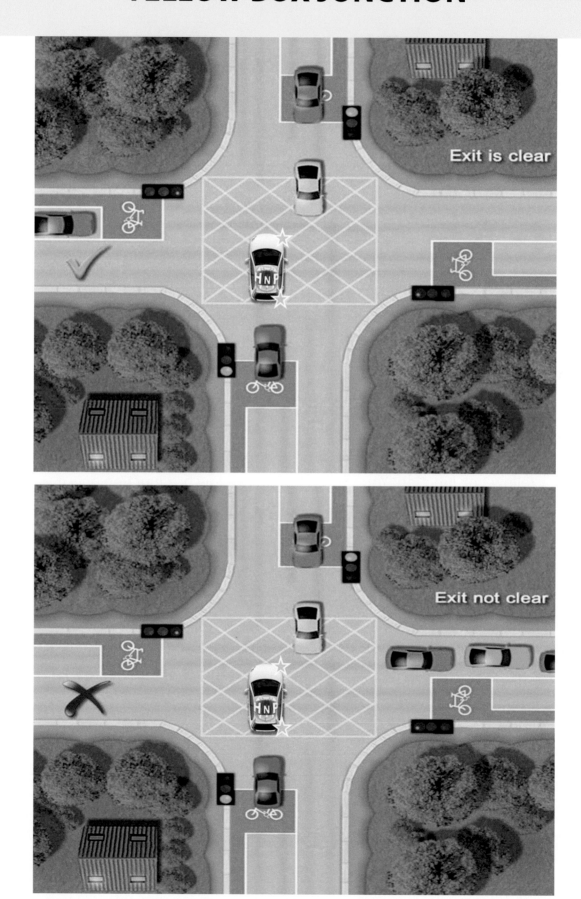

Exit is clear

Exit not clear

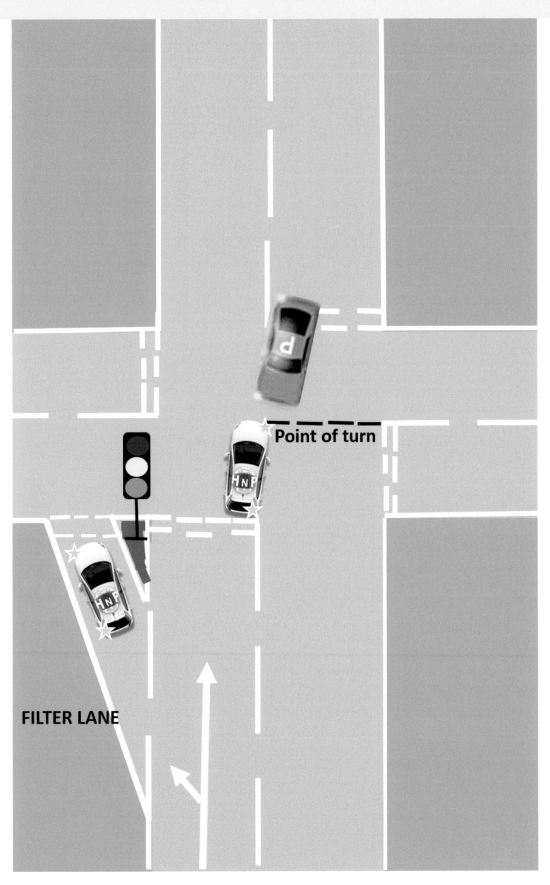

Point of turn

FILTER LANE

HALF CLUTCH / CLUTCH CONTROL

- Half clutch
- Clutch control

HALF CLUTCH / CLUTCH CONTROL

REVIEW

1. What is half clutch?
2. What is clutch control?
3. What gear do you have to be in before doing the half clutch?
4. When do you use half clutch?
5. What does clutch control enable you to do?

FACTS TO KNOW

- **Half clutch**: You half clutch when you slow down for any reason and have to drop gear from third to second. You do not take your foot completely off the clutch. You hold the clutch at the highest point of the biting point, which is the engine-braking point.
- **Clutch control**: When driving in stop-and-go traffic, you can control the speed of the car by staying in second gear instead of going into first gear. Put the clutch down if you need to slow down, and release it a little bit to generate speed if you want to move ahead. Keep doing this until you can eventually move along faster and change to third gear, or until you must stop completely and go into first gear.

TYPICAL FAULTS

- Not taking the foot high enough from the clutch to reach the biting point
- Not slowing down enough before changing gear
- Not planning ahead

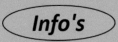

When slowing down to change to second gear, make sure you drop your speed to around 20 mph or less; otherwise, your car will jerk after you change the gear.

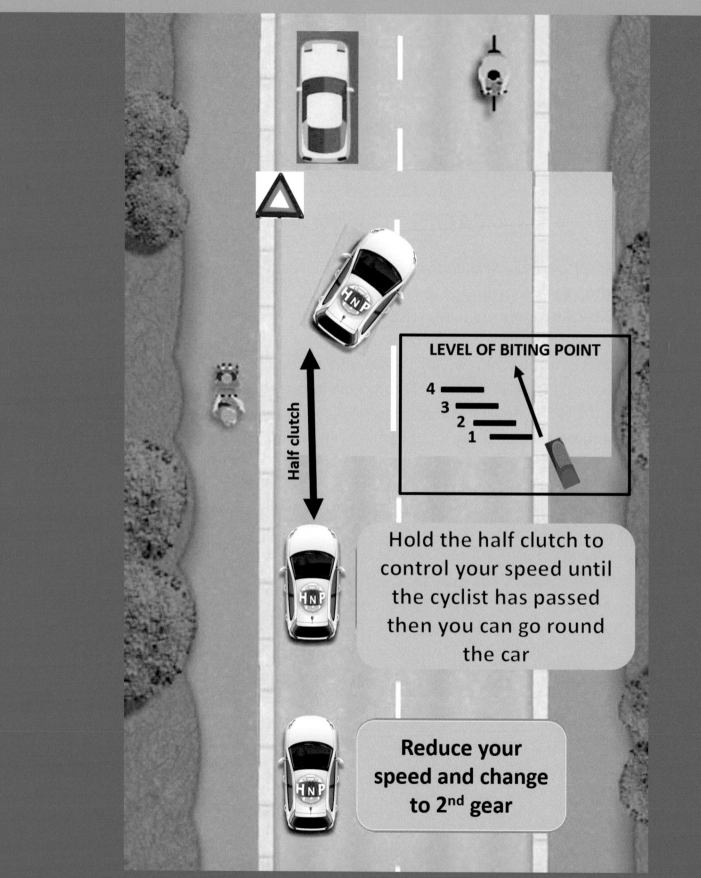

LEVEL OF BITING POINT

Half clutch

Hold the half clutch to control your speed until the cyclist has passed then you can go round the car

Reduce your speed and change to 2nd gear

MEETING

- Priorities
- Routine
- LADA (Look—Assess—Decide—Act)
- Defensive driving

MEETING TRAFFIC

REVIEW

1. What is meeting traffic?
2. What routine do you use when approaching a meeting point?
3. Who has priority when obstructions are on both sides?
4. How do you work out who has priority when no one has priority?
5. What is holdback position?
6. At how many cars' lengths do you stop behind an obstruction?
7. Where do you position your vehicle and why?
8. How do you know that the upcoming vehicle does not intend to give you priority?
9. What is defensive driving?

FACTS TO KNOW

- Meeting traffic: Any obstruction that makes the road narrow for two opposing vehicles to pass. Only one car can pass at a time.
- Routine: MSM routine and LADA routine: Look—Assess—Decide—Act.
- Priority: No one has priority (make eye contact to determine who will move first).
- Holdback position: Stop to give priority to the opposite vehicle. Stop at about two car lengths from the obstruction so you can steer less to get out and take advantage of small gaps in traffic.
- Position: Half in, half out.
- Defensive driving: Using simple tactics and techniques to stay safe and keep away from problems caused by the other road users. You will be less likely to be involved in an accident if you adopt a defensive driving style.

TYPICAL FAULTS

- ❖ Not recognising a meeting traffic point
- ❖ Not knowing who has priority
- ❖ No forward planning when approaching a meeting point
- ❖ Not checking mirrors when moving over to the right
- ❖ Stopping too close to the obstruction
- ❖ Not adopting a defensive driving style

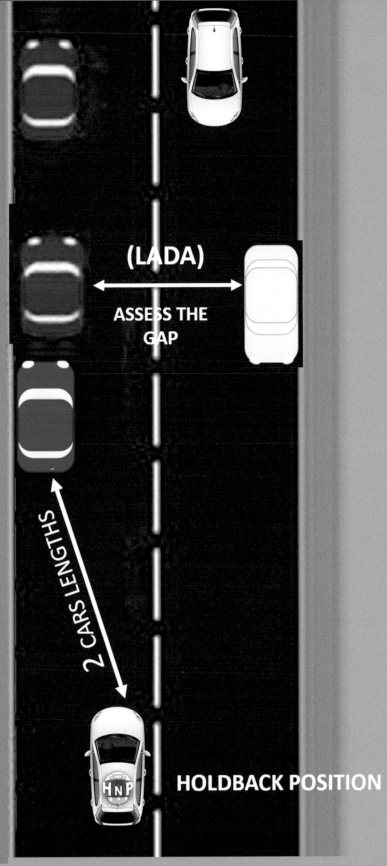

(LADA)

ASSESS THE GAP

2 CARS LENGTHS

HOLDBACK POSITION

PROGRESS

- Stopping distance
- Two-seconds rule
- Tyres and tarmac
- Pedestrians crossings

PROGRESS

REVIEW

1. What is 'tyres and tarmac'?
2. When do you apply tyres and tarmac?
3. When following a vehicle, how many seconds' gap do you observe in dry, wet, and icy conditions?
4. How do you judge the two-second gap rule?
5. Why is it important to leave extra room when overtaking a cyclist?
6. How many meters away from the kerb and middle lane you should be driving?
7. What is a pelican crossing?
8. What is a toucan crossing?
9. What routine do you use when approaching a pedestrian crossing?

FACTS TO KNOW

- Tyres and tarmac: When you stop behind a vehicle, you should be far enough away to see the two back tyres and a bit of the road.
- Following distance:
  - Dry—two seconds
  - Wet—four seconds
  - Snow—ten seconds

TYPICAL FAULTS

- Stopping too close or too far behind a vehicle
- Driving too close to the kerb
- Driving too close to the middle lane
- Not applying the two-second rule
- Driving too close when overtaking a cyclist
- Not recognizing a pedestrian crossing
- Speeding to pass a pedestrian who is approaching the zebra crossing
- Not stopping at a pedestrian crossing
- Moving before pedestrians have reached safety

PROGRESS

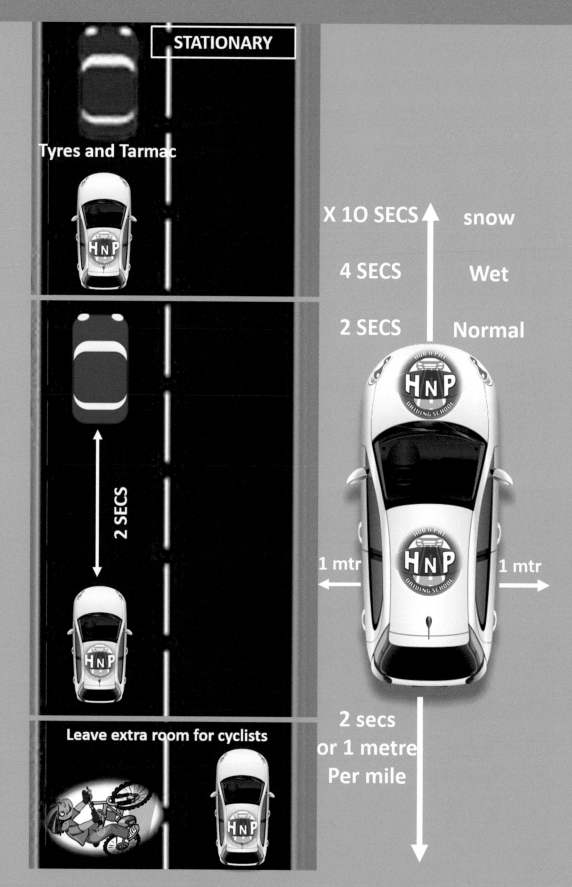

STATIONARY

Tyres and Tarmac

2 SECS

Leave extra room for cyclists

X 10 SECS — snow

4 SECS — Wet

2 SECS — Normal

1 mtr — 1 mtr

2 secs or 1 metre Per mile

PROGRESS—PEDESTRIAN CROSSINGS

PEDESTRIAN CROSSING

- KEEP CROSSING CLEAR IN TRAFFIC.
- APPROACH
- ✓ MSM ROUTINE.
- ✓ SCAN FOR PEDESTRIANS.
- ✓ STOPPING POSITION
- ✓ SECURE CAR WHEN WAITING.
- ✓ DO NOT BECKON PEDESTRIANS.

- PROCEEDING
- ✓ ENSURE PEDESTRIANS HAVE CROSSED BEFORE MOVING.
- ✓ CHECK MIRRORS.

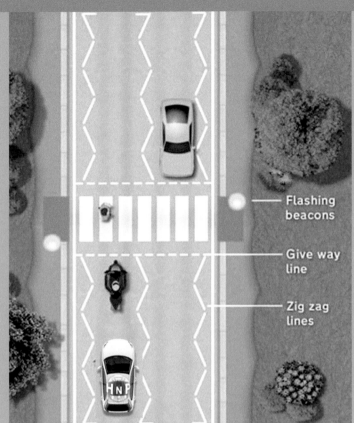

Flashing beacons

Give way line

Zig zag lines

PELICAN CROSSING

- **FLASHING AMBER**

MANNED CROSSING
- LOLLIPOP PERSON
- TRAFFIC WARDEN
- POLICE OFFICER
- STOPPING POSITION

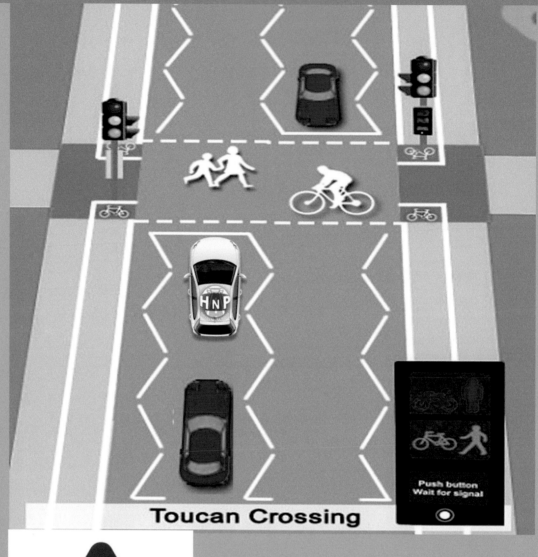

Toucan Crossing

Push button
Wait for signal

TOUCAN CROSSING SIGN

TOUCAN CROSSING

✓ **PEDESTRIANS AND CYCLIST**

ROUNDABOUTS

- Left turn
- Going straight ahead
- Right turn
- Lane discipline
- Spiral roundabout

ROUNDABOUTS

REVIEW

1. Who has priority in a roundabout?
2. What is the difference between a roundabout and a mini roundabout?
3. On a two-lane road with no markings, what is the left lane for?
4. On a two-lane road with no markings, what is the right lane for?
5. What routine do you use when approaching a roundabout?

FACTS TO KNOW

- Priority: Any vehicles already on the roundabout approaching from your right
- Lanes (no markings)
  - Left lane to turn left and go straight ahead.
  - Right lane to turn right only.
- Routine: MSPSL routine.

TYPICAL FAULTS

- ❖ Not acknowledging roundabout
- ❖ Not knowing the difference between a roundabout and a mini roundabout
- ❖ Using the wrong lane
- ❖ Not knowing who has priority
- ❖ Driving too fast when approaching the roundabout
- ❖ Poor judgement of traffic
- ❖ Stopping in the middle of the roundabout for no apparent reason

ROUNDABOUT

MINI ROUNDABOUT

Mini roundabout road sign

ROUNDABOUT—LEFT TURN

REVIEW

1. What routine do you use when turning left on the roundabout?
2. Which position do you have on a single-lane road?
3. Which lanes do you use on a two-lane road?
4. What speed and what gear do you use when approaching the roundabout?
5. Where do you look when approaching the roundabout and what are you looking for?

FACTS TO KNOW—MSPSL ROUTINE: MIRROR—SIGNAL—POSITION—SPEED—LOOK

- **Mirror**: Centre and left mirror
- **Signal**: Left signal
- **Position**:
    - Single lane: centre of the lane
    - 2 lanes no markings: Left lane
- **Speed**: 15 – 20 mph, second gear
- **Look**: Right, ahead, left, looking for a safe gap to go

TYPICAL FAULTS

- ❖ Not acknowledging roundabout
- ❖ Not knowing the difference between roundabout and mini roundabout
- ❖ Using the wrong lane
- ❖ Not knowing who has priority
- ❖ Driving too fast when approaching the roundabout
- ❖ Poor judgement of traffic
- ❖ Stopping in the middle of the roundabout for no apparent reason

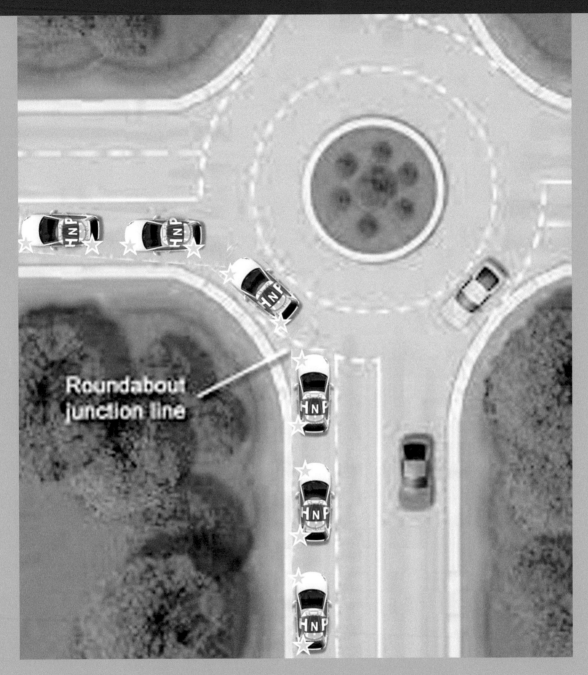

Roundabout
junction line

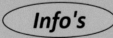 **HOW TO JUDGE SAFE GAP**

If you can walk across, you can drive across.

It's very important to assess vehicles approaching from the right. Judge their speed and their tyre direction before committing to drive ahead. Some vehicles will not signal, causing you to misjudge their direction.

ROUNDABOUT—STRAIGHT AHEAD

REVIEW

1. What routine do you use when approaching on the roundabout?
2. Which lanes do you use on a two-lane road?
3. What speed and what gear do you use when approaching the roundabout?
4. Where do you look when approaching the roundabout and what are you looking for?
5. At what point do you check your mirror and signal left?
6. Who benefit from that signal?

FACTS TO KNOW—MSPSL ROUTINE: MIRROR—SIGNAL—POSITION—SPEED—LOOK + SIGNAL

- **Mirror**: Centre and left mirror.
- **Position**:
  - Single lane: Centre of the lane.
  - Two lanes, no markings: Left lane
- **Speed**: 15–20 mph, second gear
- **Look**: Right, ahead, left, looking for a safe gap to go
- **Signal** : As you passing the first exit.

TYPICAL FAULTS

- Drifting to another lane
- Using the wrong lane
- Not knowing who has priority
- Driving too fast when approaching the roundabout
- Poor judgement of traffic
- Not checking any mirrors
- Forgetting to signal or signalling too late
- Stopping in the middle of the roundabout for no apparent reason

Info's   **LANE DISCIPLINE**

After entering the roundabout, make sure you stay on the outside lane all the way through to avoid a collision with vehicles in the right lane going right.

ROUNDABOUTS—RIGHT TURN

REVIEW

1. Which lanes do you use when turning right?
2. What speed and what gear do you use when approaching the roundabout?
3. Where do you look when approaching the roundabout and what are you looking for?
4. At what point do you check your mirror and signal left?

FACTS TO KNOW—MSPSL ROUTINE: MIRROR—SIGNAL—POSITION—SPEED—LOOK

- **Mirror**: Centre and right mirror
- **Signal**: Right signal
- **Position**: Right lane
- **Speed**: 15–20 mph, second gear
- **Look**: Right, ahead, left, looking for a safe gap to go

TYPICAL FAULTS

- Drifting to another lane
- Driving close to the island
- Using the wrong lane
- Not knowing who has priority
- Driving too fast when approaching the roundabout
- Poor judgement of traffic
- Not checking any mirrors
- Forgetting to signal or signalling too late
- Stopping in the middle of the roundabout for no apparent reason

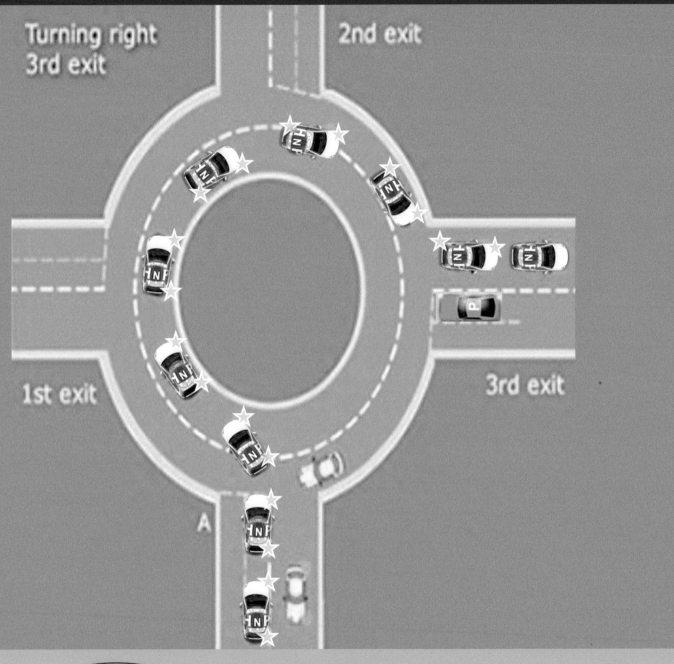

Turning right
3rd exit

2nd exit

1st exit

3rd exit

A

Info's   **JUDGEMENT**

When approaching the roundabout, look for vehicles in the right lane before making your final decision to go or stop.

Info's   LANE DISCIPLINE: THE INVISIBLE LANE

When you enter a roundabout where there is no lane marking to separate the two lines, imagine where that middle lane would be. That is the invisible lane. Stay outside it to avoid causing a collision with another vehicle.

ROUNDABOUTS—SPIRAL

REVIEW

1. How do you identify a spiral roundabout?
2. What routine do you use on a spiral roundabout?

FACTS TO KNOW

- Spiral roundabouts are very large and busy roundabouts. It's essential to learn to deal with these correctly because incorrect lane discipline could lead you cause an accident.
- Identifying a spiral roundabout: On the approach, watch for signs that indicate the layout of the roundabout. It could be arrows, words, hash marks, or dotted lines. These help you to decide which lane to be in. Quite often, the arrows point straight on. This is to prevent drivers from turning right immediately when they enter the roundabout. Don't rely on the arrows 100 per cent.
- Markings: The abundance of lane marking can be very confusing. Just focus on the ones that apply to you and ignore the rest.
- Exits and lanes: Some spiral roundabouts have four, five, or even six exits. Multiple lanes can take you to the same direction. Stay in the left lane because it will take you into your normal driving lane position. Once you are in the correct lane, stick with it and let it carry you off the roundabout.

TYPICAL FAULTS

- ❖ Not identifying spiral roundabout
- ❖ Using the wrong lane
- ❖ Drifting to another lane
- ❖ Not knowing which exit to take
- ❖ Signalling too early before the exit, confusing the other drivers
- ❖ Poor judgement of traffic
- ❖ Not checking any mirrors

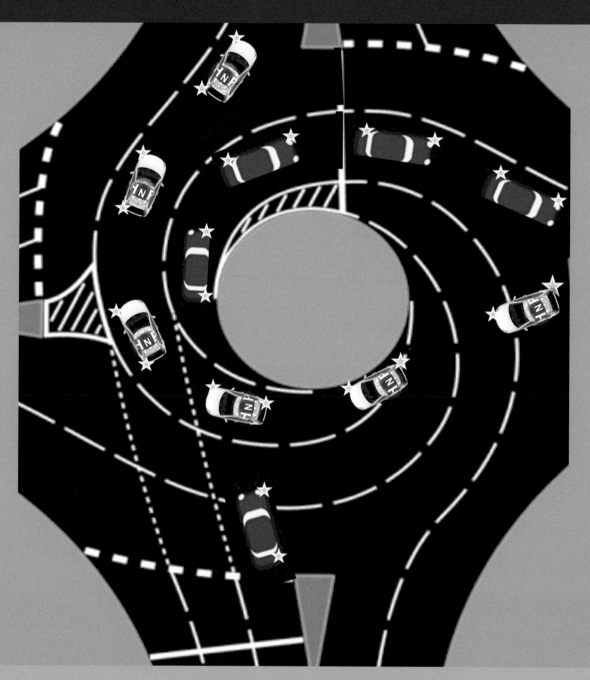

Info's **LANE DISCIPLINE**

Once you are in the correct lane, join the roundabout and stick with that lane all the way until you exit the roundabout.

Don't forget to check your centre and left mirrors and signal left as you pass the exit before yours.

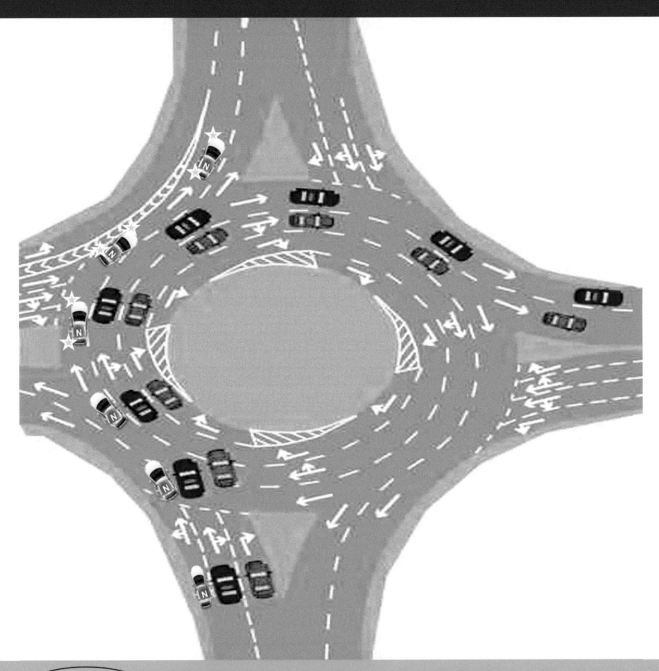

Info's   ROAD MARKING REMINDERS

The abundance of roads markings can be very confusing. Focus on the one that applies to you by following the arrow in front of you and ignoring the rest of the markings. You will be led to your exit.

Multiple lanes can take you to the same place. Always use the left because it will take into your normal driving lane position.

DUAL CARRIAGEWAYS

- Lanes
- Speed
- Centre reservation
- Slip road
- Overtaking

DUAL CARRIAGEWAYS

REVIEW

1. How do you identify a dual carriageway?
2. What is your normal driving lane position?
3. What is the right lane for?
4. Before returning to the left lane, which mirror do you look to assess the speed of the vehicules?
5. Which mirrors do you use before overtaking a slow vehicle?
6. How do you know when it's safe to come back into the left lane?
7. What is the speed on the drive carriageway?
8. How often should you look in the mirrors?
9. How does your speed impact your braking?
10. How do you plan early on a dual carriageway?
11. Why is it important to keep up with the traffic?

FACTS TO KNOW

- Identifying a dual carriageway: two lanes and speed centre reservation
- Lanes: Left lane: normal driving position

  Right lane: overtaking and turning right only
- Speed: Built-up area: up to 40 mph

  Countryside area: up to national speed limit
- Mirrors: Check every eight to ten seconds
- Overtaking: Check mirrors first and assess speed of vehicles in the right lane
- Moving back into the left lane: Check mirrors first to assess speed of vehicles in the left land and their distance from you
- Braking: Brake early and gradually because it will take longer to stop due to your speed
- Planning: Look far and up (open vision) for any hazards

TYPICAL FAULTS

- ❖ Driving too slowly on the dual carriageway
- ❖ Poor assessment before overtaking
- ❖ Moving back into the left lane too early
- ❖ Not checking any mirrors
- ❖ No forward planning and awareness
- ❖ Driving in the right lane for too long
- ❖ Not braking early enough

DUAL CARRIAGEWAYS

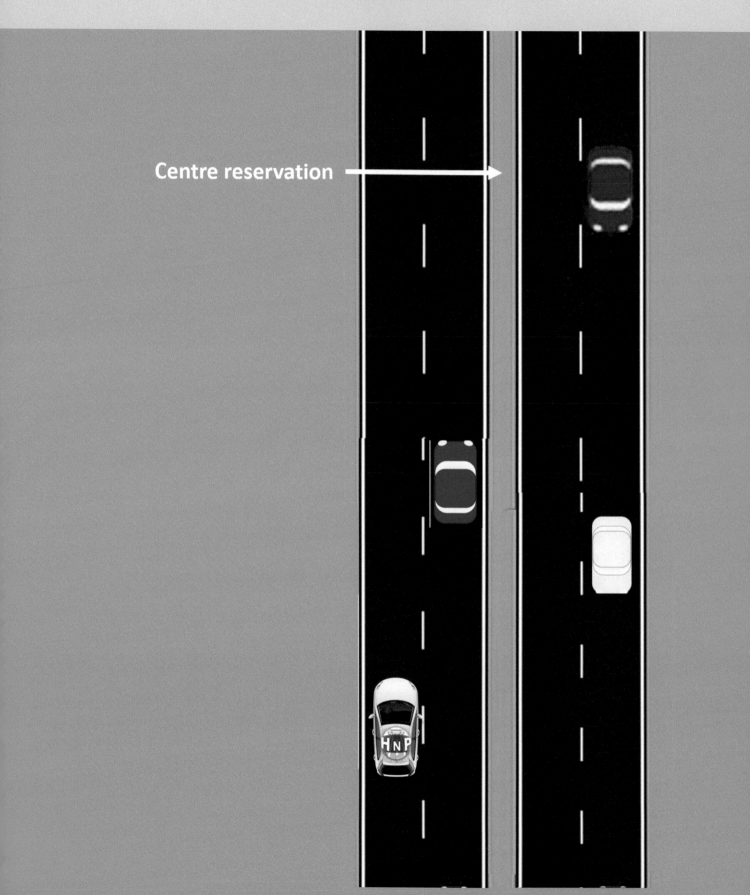

Centre reservation →

JOINING A DUAL CARRIAGEWAY

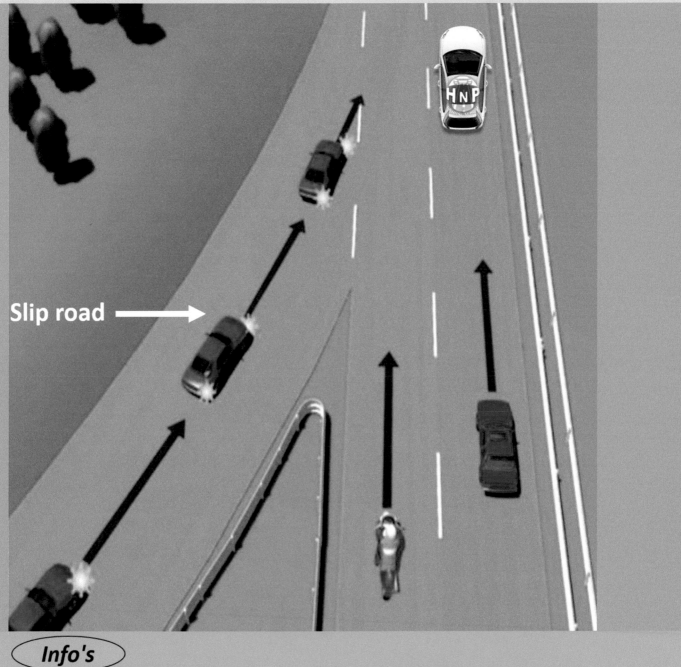

Slip road →

Info's

Joining a Dual Carriageway from a Slip Road
- Match your speed to the traffic of the lane you are joining.
- Use the length of the slip road to accelerate and use mirrors to find a gap in the traffic.
- Take a final life-saver look before you move onto the main carriageway.

MANOEUVRES

- Reverse bay parking
- Forward bay parking
- Parallel parking
- Parking on the right
- Emergency stop

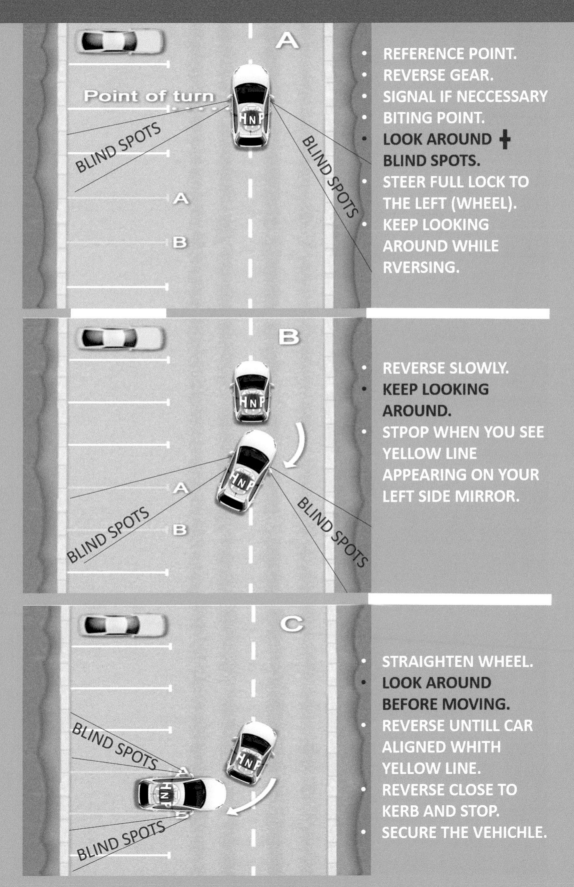

A

Point of turn

BLIND SPOTS

BLIND SPOTS

A

B

- REFERENCE POINT.
- REVERSE GEAR.
- SIGNAL IF NECCESSARY
- BITING POINT.
- **LOOK AROUND ✚ BLIND SPOTS.**
- STEER FULL LOCK TO THE LEFT (WHEEL).
- KEEP LOOKING AROUND WHILE RVERSING.

B

A

BLIND SPOTS

B

BLIND SPOTS

- REVERSE SLOWLY.
- **KEEP LOOKING AROUND.**
- STPOP WHEN YOU SEE YELLOW LINE APPEARING ON YOUR LEFT SIDE MIRROR.

C

BLIND SPOTS

A

BLIND SPOTS

- STRAIGHTEN WHEEL.
- **LOOK AROUND BEFORE MOVING.**
- REVERSE UNTILL CAR ALIGNED WHITH YELLOW LINE.
- REVERSE CLOSE TO KERB AND STOP.
- SECURE THE VEHICHLE.

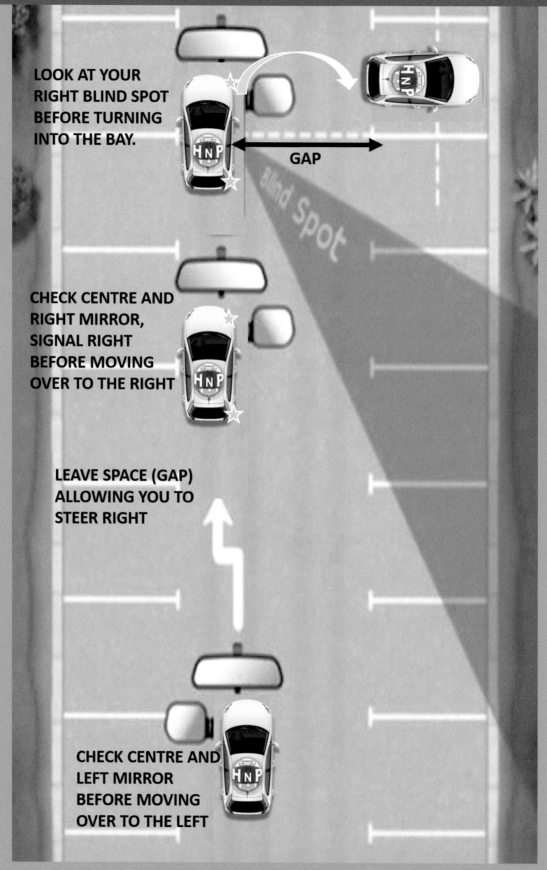

LOOK AT YOUR RIGHT BLIND SPOT BEFORE TURNING INTO THE BAY.

GAP

Blind Spot

CHECK CENTRE AND RIGHT MIRROR, SIGNAL RIGHT BEFORE MOVING OVER TO THE RIGHT

LEAVE SPACE (GAP) ALLOWING YOU TO STEER RIGHT

CHECK CENTRE AND LEFT MIRROR BEFORE MOVING OVER TO THE LEFT

MANOEUVRES — PARALLEL PARKING

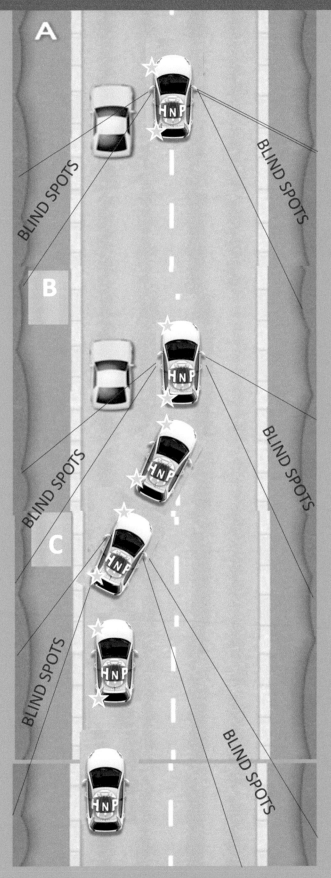

- DRIVE 1M AWAY FROM YELLOW CAR.
- REVERSE GEAR.
- SIGNAL IF NECESSARY.
- LOOK AROUND AND BLINDS SPOTS.
- RESERVE SLOWLY UNTIL YOU CAN'T SEE YELLOW CAR ON YOUR LEFT SIDE MIRROR.
- **ONE FULL TURN TO THE LEFT.**
- REVERSE UNTIL YOU CAN SEE JUST A BIT OF THE ROAD IN YOUR LEFT MIRROR.

- **TWO FULL TURN TO THE RIGHT.**
- KEEP OBSEVING ALL AROUND.
- REVERSE UNTIL BACK DOOR HANDLE IS ON THE ROAD.

- **ONE FULL TURN TO THE LEFT.**
- OBSERVE ALL AROUND.
- REVERSE STRAIGHT WITHIN TWO CARS LENGTH (INCLUDING YOUR CAR).
- SECURE THE CAR

IMPORTANT: Keep looking around including blind spots during the manoeuvre

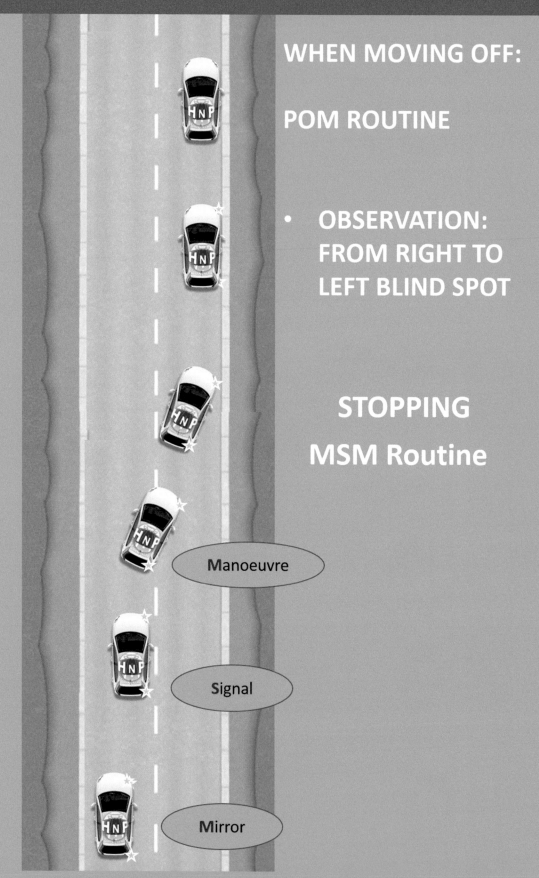

WHEN MOVING OFF:

POM ROUTINE

- OBSERVATION: FROM RIGHT TO LEFT BLIND SPOT

STOPPING

MSM Routine

Manoeuvre

Signal

Mirror

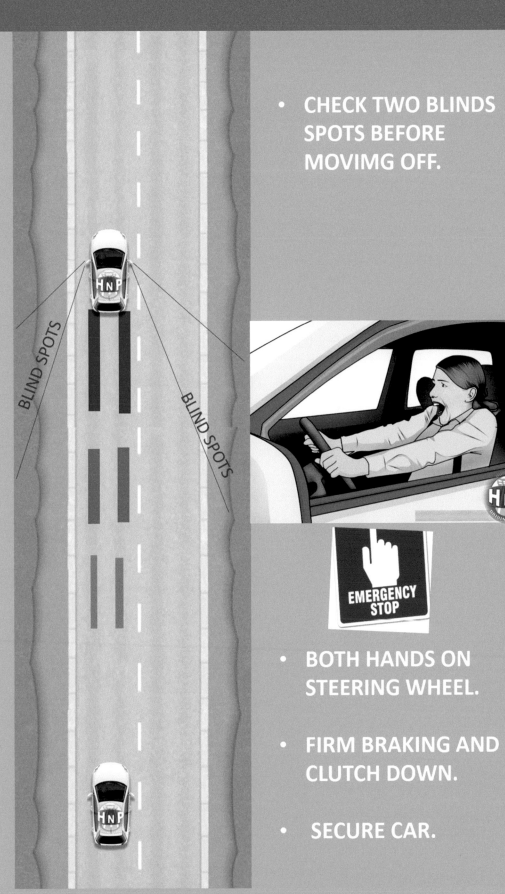

- CHECK TWO BLINDS SPOTS BEFORE MOVIMG OFF.

- BOTH HANDS ON STEERING WHEEL.

- FIRM BRAKING AND CLUTCH DOWN.

- SECURE CAR.

ANTICIPATION SKILLS

- Hazards
- Tunnel vision
- Open vision

ANTICIPATION SKILLS

REVIEW

1. What is a hazard?
2. What is tunnel vision?
3. What is open vision?
4. What type of vision should you use when driving?

FACTS TO KNOW

- **Hazard**: Something that could potentially cause harm.

- **Tunnel vision**: Your vision is narrow. You see only straight ahead and not to the sides. This can cause you to miss hazards as well as traffic signs that could help you.

- **Open vision**: You continually look far ahead as well as from side to side so that you can spot any hazards or traffic signs that might help you to plan forward.

TYPICAL FAULTS

- ❖ Not looking far enough
- ❖ Not spotting hazards early
- ❖ Not planning forward
- ❖ Not anticipating other road users' mistakes

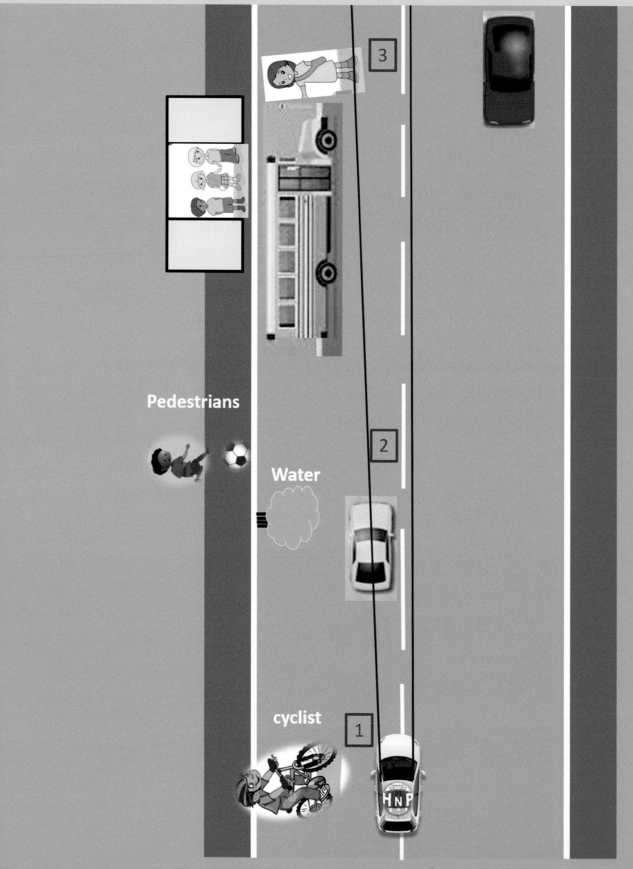

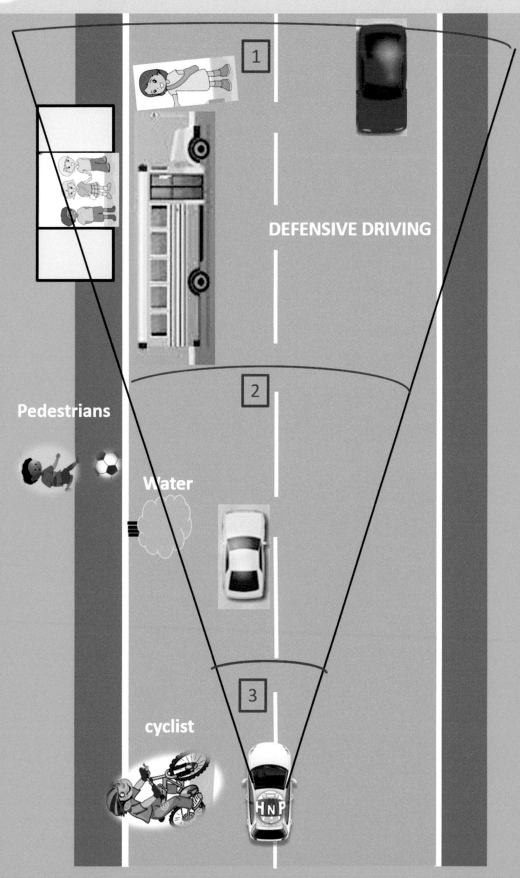

NOTES

NOTES

NOTES

This book is designed to quickly teach you all you need to know to pass your practical driving test. You will save money because you will require fewer in-person lessons.

The book contains the same knowledge that your instructor will provide and will help you understand and remember the key points of every topic. All you need to do is implement this knowledge as you practice on the road with your instructor or parents.

Use this book as you prepare for your driving test. Review it often to help you stay safe on the road.

The book includes:

✓ Eleven complete and fully illustrated lessons
✓ Questions in each section to help you measure your knowledge
✓ Knowledge sections
✓ Detailed colour illustrations for each area of focus
✓ Common learner driving faults
✓ A diary section where you can assess and log your progress

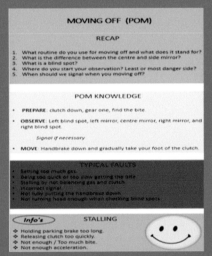
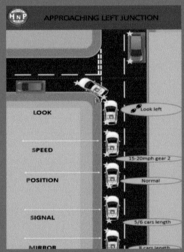
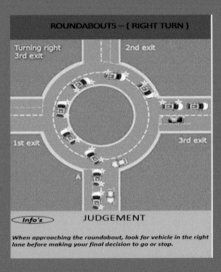

Contact

info@hubnpatdriving.co.uk

Telephone:

    0800 009 6460

On Instagram:

    @Hubnpat_driving_school

On Youtube

    @HubnPatdriving school

On Facebook:

https://www.facebook.com/HubnPat/

Printed in the United States
by Baker & Taylor Publisher Services